The Poet's Quill

The Poet's Quill

Musings of Mind and Spirit

J. MICHAELS

RESOURCE *Publications* • Eugene, Oregon

THE POET'S QUILL
Musings of Mind and Spirit

Copyright © 2009 J. Michaels. All rights reserved. Except for brief quotations in critical publications or reviews, no part of this book may be reproduced in any manner without prior written permission from the publisher. Write: Permissions, Wipf and Stock Publishers, 199 W. 8th Ave., Suite 3, Eugene, OR 97401.

Resource Publications
A Division of Wipf and Stock Publishers
199 W. 8th Ave., Suite 3
Eugene, OR 97401
www.wipfandstock.com

ISBN 13: 978-1-60608-866-1

Manufactured in the U.S.A.

to Tam and Sash,
the dearest of my beloved family

Contents

Preface xi

The Poet's Quill 1
What Will It Be 2
A Graceless Age 3
Raggedy Boy 4
Tiny Town 6
Respectabullity 7
Crap and Crud 8
One Eden Way 9
No Flaws in Me 11
The Christ Among Us 12
The Long Journey 13
One Soul to Save 15
Jonny B. Good 16
Smack Yourself in the Mind 18
Yellow Brick Road 19
Beauty By The Bay 21
Mind Pain 22
At War 23
The Hearts of Men 24
The Eye of the Needle 25
The Gift I Give 26
Freedom Flight 27
Thought Forgiven 28
I Want My Perfection Back 29
I Can See Again 30
Inside Out 31
Direction Home 33
The Divine Touch Upon It 35

Becoming Each Other 36
In Mind 37
Always Free 38
God Has No Secrets 40
It Rides On the Wings of Love 42
Bump and Grind 43
To God 44
Forever in Flight 45
The Autumn of My Soul 46
A Convenient Religion 47
King for a Day 48
The Dream 49
At My Father's Feet 51
My Truth is Better Than Your Truth 52
The Bridge 54
Spiritos 55
Areas of Self Importance 56
We Never Die 57
The Promise 58
Various Ways 59
High All the Time 60
Blind Enough To See 61
Ego Gift Declined 62
Ring of Truth 63
Brothers Without Arms 64
Mr. Obama, If You Please 65
Nothing Left To Chance 66
Skinny Sister 67
The Perfect Home 68
No Need for Need 69
As I Go 71
Those I Have Known 72
All or Nothing 73
Poet Restrained 74
Mountain of a Lady 75
Each Our Own 76
Trinity 77
Perfection Restrained 78

Simplicity of Union 79
The Last Fairy Tale 80
Naked Prize 81
One Mind 82
Love Makes Me Cry 83
Flute Divine 84
Seekers of Common Thread 85
Sacrifice Poker 86
The Forgiveness Game 87
BFF 88
Perfect Ground 89
Less Road Ahead Than Behind 90
Nothing But Oneness 91
Our Will Be Done 92
Writer, Poet, Friend 93
Alternative Fruit 94
The Tower of Babble 95
? 96
Lines of Distinction 97
Choose Again 98
I Write Like a Crazy Man 99
Providence Understands 100
The World is False 101
Ultimate Facts 102
Examples of Perfection 103
Pleasure's Mask 104
And He Says Yes 105
No More Blah, Blah, Blah 106
Heaven's Gate 107
More Than My Skin 108
Words Are Not Enough 109
Nothing Fragile Here 110
Forty Times Two 111
The Feast 112
My Only Fate 113
Metamorphosis Benediction 114
Wisdom Speaks Softly 115
Table Scraps 116

Brother Walt 117
Saying Goodbye to T&A 118
What My Soul Yearns 120
Separation Anxiety 121
Enhanced Interrogation 122
Dying to Live 123
Young Brother 125
Fair Indian Prince 126
Boss Lady 127
Poet's Doubt 128

Preface

In the year of our Lord, two thousand and eight, the dream insisted it be heard by the fitful sleeping man. That dream came in the form of a poem that would not yield to sleep. After it became obvious that arising and recording the words would be the only way to ensure any rest, the man awoke and looked at his bedside clock. It read exactly 3:33am. At that time, a tale of two brothers named, oddly enough, Nicobod and Ichobod, was born. Unknown to the dreamer and soon-to-be poet, much more than he could possibly know was also being bred.

> Nicobod and Ichobod went up the hill
> Through the valley and round the bend
> They went high and they went low
> They went to and they went fro
> From here to there they went
> Looking up but fell down
> Looking for good but evil found
> Searching for truth, looking for peace
> Til they came upon a stone
> A large obstacle in their way
> They pushed and shoved
> They pulled and prodded
> But the stone remained
> And ever will, until they know
> Where lives the stone
> And its refrain

Reluctantly written, the ode became the first of several hundred the man would write before his poems would make their way into the public domain. Strangely enough, Nicobod and Ichobod did not go to print first. The first book of poems containing their small adventure was destined to arrive after a second volume, which you now hold in your hands. In the months following the birth of the boys of similar name a series of small miracles occurred. Although more poems were destined to arrive in the sleeping state, more and more they arrived when the man was awake, usually after or during his morning meditations. Though not as insistent as the original, they came without invitation at first. A word, a title, a thought was all that foretold arrival. As the man became accustomed to the late night interruptions and the morning appearances, he began to welcome them. The man's life was inexorably changed from that point onward.

That man of course, was me. Although I had, like many men, written the occasional love poem for my wife on Valentine's Day or her birthday, this was completely different. And despite the fact that I had pursued a rather unconventional spiritual path most of my life, I was unprepared for the volume, depth, and profound nature of what was to become the center of my life. Many times over the years I have asked for guidance. Many times I have prayed for a vision or enlightenment that would validate my course. Just before one of my darkest hours was to arrive, the answer came in the form of a book. I have read hundreds, possibly thousands, of books in my life and the vast majority was of a spiritual nature. But never before had I read anything that I *knew* was true.

The book, *A Course in Miracles*, was given to me by my wife shortly before the death of my mother. Although I found it difficult to understand at first, a deep inner knowing relentlessly drove me to continue reading. The more I read, the more I was convinced I had been given a gift from a divine source. A few years later, after what was by now a daily study of The Course, my young son was murdered by a boy he once considered his best friend. I will never forget the feeling of dread as I stood at my front door facing the police who had come to call late that night. I knew, even before they said anything, that it was about Christopher and that our lives would never be the same after the next few moments. My son's violent and pointless death was the most difficult event in my life. It almost destroyed me. And I believe it would have, had it not been for my loving family and this strange new book that had taught me the true meaning of forgiveness. Had I not been able to forgive my son's killer, I would have died in the most meaningful way possible. My soul would have perished and the continued existence of my body would have meant nothing. *A Course in Miracles* taught me how to forgive and how to live. I will never again for one moment doubt its efficacy or truth.

A *Course in Miracles* is difficult for most people at first but with continued reading, becomes relatively simple. That is because, although it is radically different from conventional religions and spiritual paths, it is at its heart, simple. The primary tenet of The Course is forgiveness and how it leads to untold spiritual riches. The difference between The Course and the many other spiritual paths that advocate forgiveness is The Course's definition of the term. ACIM teaches that forgiveness is essential to spiritual growth and salvation not because our brother has harmed us and we need to be magnanimous enough to "pardon his sin". It teaches instead that the world as we experience it with our senses and perception is false. Therefore, anything done in that context is forgiven because it is illusion and a projection of the ego mind. As radical as this may seem, consider for a moment what *you* consider *real*. If we truly believe in a benevolent, all-powerful, and loving God, then how is it possible to reconcile the world as we know it with these qualities? Is it possible that God did not create the world as we know it? How could a loving God create such a foul and reckless place? Perhaps the real world *is* one of love, peace, and harmony. And maybe, just maybe, *we* made the world we experience on a daily basis. Let us consider the possibility that separation from the Oneness that must be God would leave us with a deficit that could certainly blind us to what we had traded for an individual life. In that blindness, is it possible that we made a world of separate things, a world of opposites, filled with the qualities that are antithetical to the divine nature? Maybe the *real* world is the one God created and this world is the one we made in His absence.

Rather than attempt to describe the beautiful place that I believe God created for us, I will leave that to The Course and my poems, if you choose to read them. What I can say about it is that it has changed my life; completely, profoundly, and so much for the better that my frail words cannot do it justice. So if I have yet to alienate, offend, or amuse you, please read on. I can guarantee but one thing. You won't be bored.

The Poet's Quill

I am absorbed by the poet's quill
The magic it brings
The truth it tells
Such a simple instrument
In an age so complex
So much more powerful
Than technology's bequest
A conduit for great thoughts
So elegantly expressed
Harbinger of things to come
Reminder of what has passed
The pen is truly mightier
Than sword or saber raised
Used as tribute to all that is true
Eraser of counterfeit praise

What Will It Be

What will come of this
Fair work in progress
Gleaming pen
Velvety paper
Ebony ink
Gliding so smoothly
Towards wisdom lent
It is all quite an adventure
And a great mystery to me
Perhaps someday we will see
Where journey has led us
To story or fable
To amuse and entertain
A sonnet to stir the soul
Puzzle for mind so fair
Let us travel this one together
And see how we all fare

A Graceless Age

A time of addiction
To so many things
From food to sex to drugs
To mind-numbing entertainment
We settle for so little
When we are worth so much
Sell our souls for a dollar
Or the world's nod in our favor
Exchanging so much for so little
The grandeur of the soul oppressed
Our spirit weeps at the tragedy
Of greatness lost for less
A major fish in a minor pond
Traded for ownership in the All
Given up for a pittance
Sacrificed for nothing at all
Reclaim your divinity my brother
Relinquish it no more
Resign as slave to the world
Come home as Christ reborn

Raggedy Boy

A street urchin born in filth
Hard times his accounting
Penniless often, all in tatters
Hungry more often than not
Begging for pennies his trade
Resisting the call to crime
Empty pockets but soul shining bright
The street his bed, a doorway his home
Cold and hardness his fellows
Striving each day to be a better man
While the world pressed him down
No comfort for this boy
No clothing to adorn respectable
Nothing but rags to offer cover
Nothing but darkness to hide his shame
But this man-boy would never give up
Nor let the devil buy his soul
In his heart lived goodness
His mind shone bright
But try as he may
No leave granted by his life
The hard days and long nights
Brought no comfort or delight
No reason to live, no reason to fight
One rainy morn in London town
He stayed where he slept
The soul light dimming
The body now eager to die
All hope seemed lost now
No balm for his courage, all but gave out
But the day was not done
In alley so damp and dark
Our boy had left but one request
The one thing still held dear

He longed to ask it
But no one there to hear
With nothing to lose he voiced it
A prayer departed his lips
Dear Father please grant me
This one last wish
Take this mouse from my pocket
And grant the life I give up
Be kind to this tiny creature
May he find love and a home
Not mine to grant or loan
Dear Lord, take him for your own
He died not knowing but soon discovered
The Lord always claims his own

Tiny Town

Greater messages may be withered
To retreat to stricter limits
Given just enough specificity
To confirm what we want to believe
Who needs all that extraneous stuff
When the world is all we see
A grander reality lost from view
The siphoning process begins
Funneled down to a smaller actuality
Seemingly safer than the Whole
But in truth we lose too much
That without the meaning intact
We think we have arrived
And arrived we have, at Tiny Town
Settling for dirt floors
With perfect skies overhead

Respectabullity

Let no rules justify
The judging of another
For we are all connected
Whether judge or jury be
Whether prosecutor or plaintiff
We judge ourselves included
With guilt our only pay
The guilt is self-breeding
Provide it no place to stay
So if your code exceeds your love
Then neither serves you well
The one most never will
The other will never fail
So cast off the cloak
That so respectfully adorns
The image held in mind
Of those socially acceptable norms
Look inward to start your search
For the truly authentic who
Never again settle for less
Than the simplest you

Crap and Crud

My friend here
Cuts through all the crap
With a velvety razor
The softest of edges
The cleanest of cuts
Through the layers of resistance
To the core of the crud
That which imprisons
And tortures our soul
Veils invisible and subtly placed
In line of sight of our true selves
Beyond which lives the origin
That gave us what we prayed
For the veils to melt away
Leaving grace in its stead
Cutting through all the bullshit
Setting sails for Heaven's gate

One Eden Way

Oneness once ours
And always is, once found
We see what apart did for us
Witness the world in all it seems
Yet we are perfect beings
Who lived at One Eden Way
Someone left the door ajar
In crept the mad idea
Determined much to stay
We entertained it slightly
Then gave it leave some more
The perfect Being entertaining
The one imperfect thought
In Eden we had everything
And there resides no fear
In this our Home, we lived in freedom
To think of what we may
A single mistake we made that day
We desired to be our own god
But to pull aside from all there is
Is such a case of folly
That we never should have thought it
And never invited it in
The thought of perfection exceeded
With little me in charge
So change we did
Our primary residence
Heaven for the world
Chaos for perfection
Such guilt as is hard to imagine
Our inheritance that day
Blinding our eyes
Deafening our ears
To truth, now in the background
So welcome to earth

And the play we so excitedly perform
Dare we turn around and think
Of what a return to Home would be
Would the gates re-open
Would my Father greet me there
I think I'm going to try it
I think I want to feel
Exactly like I used to be
And somehow always will
I think I know the answer
To the biggest question of all
It starts with "Who am I?"
And ends with "Where should I be?"
My Father in all His glory
Greets me at Eden's gate
And says to me in magnificent voice
Welcome Home My Son
It's good to be Us again

No Flaws in Me

A decree so difficult to imagine
An assertion of magnificent appeal
A goal worthy of us all
But climb no fences
Nor towers or bridges
Nothing to accomplish
Nothing to do
Simply being who we are
With no fences, towers, or bridges
Encompassing those and more
Leaving no room for gap or divide
Part of that perfect something
Jointly owned and housed inside

The Christ Among Us

Costumed in body
Attending the grand masquerade
Hidden below the surface
Without leave to unmask, He fades
Imprisoned we are
By mind's heavy chains
Refusing to see Him
Or hear His holy refrain
Invincible, He waits
For the moment of our arrival
Appearing at glory's gate
Ready to be done with
All that blocks the light
Ready now to be
The Christ for all to see

The Long Journey

Baby steps first taken
Freed from mommy's arms
First traces of the journey
Even as infant it moves her on
Toddler on nameless quest
Questions without yet knowing
What teetering steps will bring
Or where she may be going
Body growing taller and stronger
Steps pacing faster and longer
Increasing the tempo towards nameless goal
Driven by needs unknown
Searching blindly for what she seeks
Failing to understand what she yearns
Never knowing who to follow
Yet the urge drives her on
From person to place to thing
Still looking for the answers
To what her life will bring
Emerging as woman and looking about
Inside meager belongings
Soundly distracted by occasion
Hoping that time will inform
Method to satisfy the equation
Looking through eyes of another
Perchance window to lend a clue
Why does she search so madly
What price for confidence due
Perhaps a new vehicle to deliver her
Or will this verse inform the truth
Will meaning arrive from service
Or by running swiftly in pursuit
Wiser, stronger, now on her own
Still looking for ultimate answer
Career and capital don't quite do it

Husband and kids decline the breach
Her life lacks such fullness
As she would strive to reach
In time aged woman emerges
Wondering what she must do
To find herself in this lonely world
Where on earth are alluded clues
She sees that she really must know
Before the last breath is drawn
To make her life complete and whole
Before the final dawn
She refuses to die without it
The answer to ancient fears
At last she thinks she may have it
Maybe death will loosen the riddle
Of whom she is and where she belongs
Between cradle and darkened grave
All these years and still no clue
Of rightful purpose or place
One dismal day, furrowed and older
She considers the choice to make
She decides lastly to look inside
Searching for path to take
The dilemma at hand to live or die
Choice now made and fate decided
She waits for final answer
An instant before death arrives
Her longing parts the veil
Father's love comes welcomed in
Her mind awakes after years of slumber
And in that moment was granted
The reply to all her appeals
The ones she oft repeated
And those she never revealed
All provided at once
In words rightly unspoken
Journey finally over
When Christ is known as real

One Soul to Save

There is but one soul to save
No crusades to foreign lands required
No sermons to preach
No baptism needed
No rules to impose or follow
Little instruction in this curriculum
No training for the soul
Only love let in essential
To recover what was never forsaken
The state of grace our natural place
We possess all that is needed
Shed the lessons of the world
Unveil the soul prior saved
Not yours or mine I talk about
No unique requirement in place
The soul we seek and inquire regarding
Is the one we all share in grace
Our Father created but single Son
A sole spirit before the fall
And find we will
And recover we must
The only Soul saved for All

Jonny B. Good

Jonny B. Good was a rock star
Adored and cheered by many
A gift for music lived within
Treasure of his soul to share
His voice lent accompaniment
The guitar sang in perfect balance
The lyrics voiced so well
The thrill of the adventure and excitement
Flailed young Jonny about
Not knowing whether coming or going
The world tilting in various ways
Pleasures and seductions surrounded
The candy store quite full
Of sundry treats and goodies
To tempt the boy to fate
Jonny sang and played his tunes
To crowds who yelled and screamed
Then off to parties afterward
To numb the growing need
Young girls quite willing and available
To please and resolve the need
But bodies were not what Jonny hoped for
The booze and drugs no longer worked
The emptiness that grew inside him
Not deterred by any party favor
Still he accepted the hollow offerings
Hoping enough would fill his cup
But the more he took the less he became
Knowing his life would end some day
He hoped his legacy would be
Much more than he had accumulated
More to offer for what he had become
The music his only salvation
The one pure thing he played
The only thread from soul to man

To keep Jonny alive and sane
After awhile even the music dimmed
The light fading from his heart
Jonny B. Good was dying
Only his body left in sight
One morning he awoke
In pool of vomit and gin
So very much to be sick about
His life reduced to this
But Jonny knew he was more than this
Better than what he had become
Something still lived within his soul
Yearning to sing its song
So Jonny lifted his head and cried
The tears purifying the mess
That symbolized the life he had led
But never would again
He took his last cleansing as rock star
Alone with just his soul
Knowing his music would save him
His Father, now his only Muse

Smack Yourself in the Mind

Snap out of it my friend
Smack yourself in the mind
Get out of the daze you're in
Look within and you will find
Wonders to amaze you
Lovely things unimagined
Heavenly delights all around you
Far exceeding what is known now
The world that daily distracts us
A shadow of the one that attracts us
A shallow pond, a hollow enticement
With all its seeming pieces
All trying to fit together
No union for the body
No peace for the soul
We've tried for what seems like forever
To fail forever, the goal
No union on earth dear fellows
Only Paradise makes us whole

Yellow Brick Road

Stuck again in traffic
With all my fellows on wheels
Driving home from long day's labor
Inching along on each other's heels
Vehicles proceed in slow motion
The speed not the trouble
The time matters not
What amazes me this day
Are the pieces in total
The parts all apart
Frail bodies on cushioned seats
Metal steeds on high speed threads
Moving along, scarcely in unison
Struggling to act as one
Constant adjustment of speed and motion
Hoping to avoid dire collision
Let us look beyond the rutted way
For that which unites us well
A golden road neither crowded nor divided
With nothing opposed or apart
This byway leads us somewhere special
Grander than dinner at days end
A mundane life soon becomes habit
Leaving us to wonder where we've been
Perhaps we can take a different tact
And see what daily eludes us
A look into a better place
Than dashboard or tail lights afford
A simple need to close the eyes
Deny the obvious around us
Let sublime reality intrude
On rational thought that delays us
For all we believe and all we sense
Are but parlor tricks to confuse
And partition our sight and knowing

Into separate people, beliefs, and views
Riding on separate byways
Homeward bound to find some accord
Let us try a different vehicle
One we can rightly afford

Beauty By The Bay

Fair city aside the bay
Ocean breezes to cool the way
Crowds bustling among city streets
Riding the Bart above
Through subterranean byways below
Cable cars amid glass and steel
Money changers making deals
Fine food and wine available
For those who close the deal
Material finery at its best
Ocean painted as backdrop
Making us all feel quite important
To be among the American elite
Attractions and beauty abound
To amuse and bedazzle all day
Distracting from the crack below us
Poised to swallow all it may
Fear not dear Californians
I share your love of the place
For we have a friend in higher places
Who loves us no matter our fate

Mind Pain

Pain, my constant companion
A puzzle of mind to brain
Unable to see just cause
For long-suffering with modest gain
But I know as sure as I stand here
All disease is self-inflicted
All that ails the body
Born of the mind's thinking way
Sigmund saw the light
Dr. Jung knew it too
All that hurts and plagues us
Fruit of the mind come true
Separation in mind got it started
Continued on in time and place
Manifest as all sorts of things
Guilt-driven to stay that way
The body shows only symptoms
No cause for the neutral toy
Mind always in charge
Of peace and pain and joy

At War

Our wars are far from uncommon
On earth, a natural state of affairs
Why is it they surprise us
War has always been the game plan
In a world divided so
A place inherently unstable
What else could be our course
Conflicting on so many levels
Part of our daily lives
The war that rages within
Manifests in all we see
The marriage filled with strife
To the family torn apart
By arguing and fighting
Battles among our lives
Communities and towns at odds
With ideologies as knives
Cutting apart our oneness
Fueling the fires of war
Our states and nations the same
As they face off armor-bound
Each so sure of their position
Destined for glory found
Patriotism and nationalism
Merely ways to fire the troops
Of men, boys, and women
To strike at brothers hearts
So look not to foreign policy
Or larger armies still
Look within our hearts dear brothers
For treaties place and wars end

The Hearts of Men

Within the heart of men
Centered in the core of life
Lies all of life's secrets
The remedies for our strife
The heart in truth is made of Mind
Eternal, one, and true
And in that place that knows no limits
Lives our world in faintest blue
A part of mind propelled by guilt
Derived from the original mistake
Taking leave of God and Heaven
Trying to make true the fake
That tiny part projects our world
At levels small and large
Reflection of the notion
That God is not our Heart
Yet the larger Mind still belongs
To us, Christ, and Creator
Holding within the treasure
That awaits the golden key
The key is where, you ask
And this is what I say
Look beyond the separation
In God's hand is found the way
He offers all we relinquished
When smaller mind was made
A significantly false impression
That we were all we need
This lilliputian mind we made
A false thought finely attired
But still no more than illusion
A lie we need no more
So look to the true heart of man
The gift that God bestowed
And live and know within that place
Where holiness is found and owed

The Eye of the Needle

Gather your wits about you
Resign as victim to life
Pull your thoughts together
Gather up all that is fine
Then shed all that covers you
All that would weigh you down
Go naked to the river
But watch, for obstacles abound
Steer naught but a truer course
Coming to point of departure
But first present and then decline
To circumvent and avoid any longer
Resign instead to become
Smaller than nothing
And larger than life
Tiny enough to align and enter
The eye of the needle and arrive
Free floating and safe
In sweet Paradise's place

The Gift I Give

My life has become poetic
Now that I've arrived at me
Found my true calling at last
To live as I now speak
For the receipt and scribing
Require a contract of sorts
Agreement to live what I teach
And to learn how I must live
To all those blessed souls
It is my honor to serve
I serve you now dear brother
No secrets, no doors, no barriers
I elect to build or maintain
Only the clues in poetic form
Given as gifts to make us sane

Freedom Flight

I have never felt so free before
Bound lightly by body and world
An inner dove set free at last
To soar to clouds above
Searching endless skies
Seeking the sun at its core
Flying about in total freedom
The winds mine to explore
Wings require no effort
Soaring as an eagle roams
The infinite my nest and home
Earth below still yields attraction
Gravity seeking to draw me down
Pulling the bird of lightness
Back again to hollow ground
Father, please don't let it land me
On rock, or river, or plain
Once a bird always a bird
Never to be grounded again

Thought Forgiven

I forgive myself
The unforgivable thought
The one that cost my freedom
The one that lost my home
But just like all the others
Created then and since
Only in dreams are they cast
Momentary figments at best
Never will they last
The punishment I give to my person
Was to be a person instead
Of living as God intended
Forgiven and never dead
The one errant thought eluded me
I chased it clear to earth
Only to awake and know
There was no cause for leaving
No reason to depart my home
A thought in dreams forgives
Before it leaves its own

I Want My Perfection Back

I want my perfection back
I'm so tired of being lifeless
So weary of being still here
A dweller on the threshold
A seeker still unfound
Wanting my home and Creator
Leaving the rest behind
The place I seek and call my home
Is so close, I truly know it
All the ones I love
Live there is spirit clothed
I'm so tired of living this dream
When I know so much awaits me
Death will not open the door
My life must grant the key
Just show me heavenly Father
All that you would have me be
All that will grant me license
To leave this place forever
Journey home completed
Perfection reinstated by Thee

I Can See Again

I want no more than I am
I need no more than is given
By the holy hands of my brother
From the heart of my Father
I relinquish my sightlessness
All my coverings too
Seeking only to find
That which has meaning and truth
I claim my sight restored
To see past all that I made
The world of illusion behind me now
Vision cleared of all not real
True sight reclaimed
Blindness repealed

Inside Out

Changing this world we live in
Is like trying to blindly alter
Pictures on a screen before us
Projected from a distant source
Like watching a story about our lives
And trying to make it different
By changing the images presented
To form the superior plot
Attempting to draw different actors
By coloring performance and dress
The frustration of life then comes
From such vain attempts to address
Ourselves and the world around us
Instead of working inside out
Much like the film of images
Put forth on silver screen
No way to change our lives
Without edit of source performed
So let us vow to cease our struggle
To control and change what is without
And look instead to the projector within us
And the story it tells us about
For our mind is that projector
And the film our very thoughts
That projected out upon our lives
Showing us what we have sought
And demonstrate beliefs unrecognized
About ourselves and others
Revealing to us our truest thoughts
Unknown until we show them
Know this about this tale
Shown upon the screen of life
It tells us what lives within us
And thoughts that drive our lives
So change we must

This we all know
To find that happy route
Change our minds we must
To improve the inside out

Direction Home

So much that constrains us
We do not even see
Thoughts and beliefs within us
Telling us what we must be
Denial, the enemy that precludes us
From seeing us as we are
Hiding the beliefs that bind us
And keeping us divided so far
Remove the blinders and you will see
What lies beneath and drives us
To make a world and life of pain
To imprison within misery's gain
Recognize and admit our error
That the world we see and feel
Is nothing more than illusion
Driven and made by fear
Fear that we are less worthy
Of Perfection that creates us all
Absorbed in guilt that belies us
To know that God is real
He created us all as perfect
Sons of the one true God
The only source that births us
The only choice that is true
We are in fact, my brothers
Sons and citizens of Heaven
Let us deny our birthright no longer
Let us deny this world instead
Made by us apart from love
Chosen by delinquent thought
The fall from Eden no myth
We truly left our home
But only in dreams did we do so
In Mind we shall return
So know that Paradise is not the illusion

But the world made without love
We have but to leave it behind us
Seeking direction only from above

The Divine Touch Upon It

The Divine reaches down and touches
With the lightest point of contact
Whatever it deems needing
Of love's adornment
Touching the inside of nothing left out
Emblazon it through heart and mind
With love's gentle coming
The grail is filled near complete
Returning home, the gift to my Father
The golden drop that levels the cup
And bids us go no farther

Becoming Each Other

Becoming each other
Sure would put sex to shame
The two into one a shining promise
Ours to reach out and be
Walls will need to crumble
Defenses require retreat
Forgiveness the order of the day
Connection promising swift arrival
Giving no time to pray
For the All-ness, our long-known heritage
For the vision to show the way

In Mind

I have deemed myself
A worthy channel at last
Sweeping away the final remnants
Of sin's annoying decay
Realizing once and forever
I never belonged that way
The body, the mistaken temple
Pales in the light of day
To the Mind in all its glory
A tepid shadow in sun's way
God is Mind
And we are Mind
The rest simply projection
Discard false addresses
Come home with me to find
All that deems us worthy
As tenants proud to reside
In sweet home of Mind

Always Free

The choice I make now
Is most profound
To be successful in the dream
Or to be free of it
I've lived in Plato's cave
It has been my dream locale
Hidden behind Oz's curtain
The wish left unrequited
Playing in a world quite congested
With things and places and lies
When backstage I hung in chains
Not knowing I was bound
Held not by shackles in truth
But only by those of mind
The smaller mind convincing the larger
A prisoner I should be
When all those years presented
I thought I was truly free
To roam in a world imprisoned
Finally peeking beyond the veil
To see myself tattered and worn
Chained to the wall with my brothers
In tears and hopelessness and pain
But pay heed my brothers
For the scene behind the scene
Is no truer than that presented
A lie still lying unseen
For a stage is still a stage
No matter the myth played upon it
These chains we believe will bind us
Have no power at all
They are but shackles of the ego mind
Used as props for its deadly play
To try and convince us
We are less than divine

And can be enslaved
Believe it not for it is a lie
We are the holy Son of God
No chains may hold us in either dream
The bonds removed by Hand of God
Showing us we were always free

God Has No Secrets

When there is nothing to fear
Then fear is nothing
Only a vaporous veil
Lowered in vain attempt
To hide truth from eyes nearly blinded
Only the world must have secrets
For only body and ego have need
To hide the lie of differences
That work so hard to deny
The oneness of true identity
Of those born of Christ
The day we finally know
And the moment we finally see
That we are in truth the whole
Of all eternity
In the brilliant moment
All will be revealed
The lying veil will evaporate
And reveal the simple secret
That being part of everything
Is being all the same
What could we possibly want
Who could we possibly hate
For in the eve of the dawning
Truth proposes to reveal
All in One is not only possible
But truly all that is real
To know we must see
That all of fear and secrecy
Never born of beloved Creator
Made merely to conceal
All that is true and calls us
To return to what we will
And to that final destination
We travel arm in arm

Brothers the same and eternal
Bound for Paradise together
Free from secret's harm

It Rides On the Wings of Love

Airy breeze barely touching
Precious face of God
Wafting then the sweet fragrance
As love flows into love
Our honor to even think of it
Dearest blessing to know
That what we are in truth
We can surely believe is so
In truest place at Heaven's door
We deliver our ticket for entry
Made of love invited in
Leaving no room for lesser tenant
The sight of our Father
Making the vision complete

Bump and Grind

Bumping into each other
As we go our separate ways
Doing things quite similar
But doing them in different ways
Some simultaneously
Some on the same day
A few for free
Some must pay
Most staying mute
A few need say
Where do we go from here
In parallel likely
But who can say
We could decide on convergence
We could decide to stay
Apart running parallel
From day to day
Time to pause and think about it
Decide now quickly
Go or stay
I'm tired of getting bumped and jostled
By another me in my way

To God

I know I'm not home yet
But I can feel its glow
Approaching slowly and surely
To all that I would know
Paradise is my home my friend
And surely yours as well
Let us help each other along the way
Let us be together as we pray
For the golden gates to swing wide
And invite us in again
This time around we know much better
This time around we mend
The fences slightly broken
By one decision off-track
Raise our eyes to the blessed vision
As God our Father welcomes us back

Forever in Flight

Names have always seemed
To be superfluous to me
Looking like an arbitrary barrier
To communication newly born
The words themselves
A necessary evil
As long as thought is blocked
By guilt or rage or fear
The melding of thought to such
Builds mind fences for sure
So sweep the room
Let in the light
Tear down the cobwebs
Leave nothing in sight
Forgive ourselves and each other
Let us know oneness
Forever in flight

The Autumn of My Soul

Autumn to me is commencement
Of journey to the threshold
Dressed in wondrous and varied color
Clothed in spiritual finery
Preparing to meet my Creator
In Sunday's best go-to-meetin clothes
The gifts are similar
In color and hue
The content much deeper
In paradise blue
Feeling my finest
In such a long time
Full color expressed
In majesty's best

A Convenient Religion

Like the pirates of Barbary
With self-interest to gain
Needed a way to legitimize
The taking of plunder and pay
The need to convince wayfaring souls
Building an army of believers
Striving to convince enough hungry minds
That doctrine will save the day
Soon no one cares or remembers
Why congregation was unavoidably so
And what religion ought to contain it
Or why we entertained it so
Is it just a way of believing
That which clings to men's hearts
Attached by media and gurus alike
With audience and believers taking part
While truth gets cloaked and rarely seen
When rules and fragile convictions converge
Trapped in belief halls so narrow
Requiring a convenient religion to restore
And tome to carry its lore

King for a Day

All the striving for power
And jockeying for position
To gain the world's silver throne
And the plastic crown it offers
Only to be king for a day
In a world composed of nothing
Political party or violent coup
Different means to common end
To be king of the hill for a moment
To make a dent in artificial history
All the crimes against brothers
Costly passage to pay to rule
But to gain this high position
Requires but living low
And giving up on the love we owe
To sit upon the throne
So when the campaign is over
When the palace is won
Don't look too hard my brother
Or you will find you rule
An empty land and little else
For the foul means employed
Never justify the end achieved
They are but excuses contrived
To justify what we seek
False concepts to cover the damage
Done to brother and soul as one
The price to be paid is much too high
It will bankrupt the treasury won
For nothing the world offers
Justifies its cost in any way
To be its top dog for an instant
Requires your soul to pay
A price far higher than imagined
To be its king for the day

The Dream

I dreamed I fell from place on high
Broke the One into many
Believed I had left my Source
Accepted division as real
Allowed the ego a separate world
Populated with beings apart
All the time projecting upon it
What I feared the most
And believed was in my heart
Supposed I betrayed my Father
By splitting off from what was whole
And leaving the state of Nirvana
To pursue the lone self's goal
It hurt me so I could not tolerate
The shame for what I had done
Regret over leaving everything
To live in a world undone
Discovered what I had relinquished
To abide among hate and fear
Too much for my soul to take
My mind bent down in pain
To survive I learned to forget
And live in the world I made
Remembering what I had left and lost
Simply too much to retain
I consented to live in illusion
Moved my belongings to the dream
Lived my varied lives in desperation
Yet in my depth I could not forget
The Heaven exchanged for hell
Driven incessantly and forever
To reclaim all thought lost
Then one bright day after many
My soul did remind me well
That all I thought I surrendered

Happened only in dream of hell
I awoke knowing
My Father never left me
And that I had been asleep
For countless years and lifetimes
Spent acting in the endless play
My brother Christ comforted
My tired and aching soul
Introduced me to the Holy Spirit
Who had come to make me whole
They both said unto me
To lay down fear and remorse
The prodigal son has returned at last
It was time to join and rejoice
My brothers in Christ assembled
There to welcome me home
And present me to my Father
Who smiled with unbridled joy

At My Father's Feet

I am no longer fragmented
I know I belong to the Whole
Never again to be estranged
From the oneness of my soul
Forgotten is the state of being alone
I know it was never true
Always a part of my Father
Never having left my home
I know there is nothing
To fear or be guilty about
My Creator has never condemned me
For what I thought I left out
My mind wandered but for an instant
Into hell that seemed eternal
But now I am back to the place never left
And the joy that fills me once more
Safe and free, whole and complete
Sitting in peace at my Father's feet

My Truth is Better Than Your Truth

Obviously, you misunderstand me
When I tell you what must be told
You are quite sadly mistaken
To believe what you hold true
For my little piece of reality
Exceeds the one you possess
I must be right while you are wrong
Let it be proven by simple test
I have more in stock than you
My credentials quite impeccable
My clarity far superior
To the cloud that surrounds your head
Your station in life far below me
Your ignorance quite evident
My intelligence puts me ahead
So obvious it is to everyone
That I must be your assigned superior
So you might as well bequeath me
Your meager belongings as well
Some day you will awake and thank me
For showing you what was true
Bringing you over to my way of thinking
Bestowing awareness of how little you know
So accept your tiny fate
Simply acknowledge all I have done
And accept my ultimate certainty
For now I am sure you can see
How much better my truth than yours

Heed not this voice of boisterous ego
That seeks to demean and degrade
This voice hides within us
Taking this form or that
But know we must, it is not the truth
For there is only one

It comes from sweet Creator
And applies to all his brood
You will know it by its nature
And the love that calls it home
With forgiveness complete within it
The one Truth that is our own

The Bridge

From here to there crossing over
A bridge before us appears
Light upon its wooden timbers
Inviting us to travel there
The crossing, a gap behind us
The bridge spanning the divide
That keeps us apart and contested
No longer victim to the falling
Emergent from the chasm below
Reaching to set foot in the garden
That leads us to where we need go
The world behind, an illusion denied
Truth waits on destined side
Take the bridge we will
My brothers of similar fate
Gather again on the other side
Assemble at perpetuity's gate

Spiritos

I coax a breeze from the spiritual wind
Gently sliding along my skin
Peace, a silent partner in the coming
Gentle hand upon my heart
Feel the pulse of life expanding
Spiritos forever unending
The comfort of home consults me
Leaving extraneous items alone
Left only with its essence
Spiritos grinning at the greeting
Incomplete for years unending
Lost since time began
Now turned around and ready to go
Spiritos revealed again

Areas of Self Importance

Self importance wears a burly coat
To keep beliefs from wandering
Firmly convinced that all should see
What makes him special and prince
Armed with something to turn the tide
Convincing others of his worth
Himself, the true non-believer
Yet fear demands a price
To be paid in guilt and denial
Enhancing the image presented
In hopes of awe and regret
From audiences who coveted his
But must settle for less at best
Challenge not his self image
Nor critique his pain
His areas of self importance
Leaving nothing left to gain
Until the life force leaves him
A compacted ego remains

We Never Die

Though I may someday soon
Lay this body down
The end of a dream will dawn
And by my Father's grace
Another will cease to be
I know now and ever will
Who I am and where I live
Forever in the heart of love
Forever in my Beloved One
I have no cause for worry
Or death to fear or avoid
The dream of the form will fade
The light of my soul will stay
Eternally where it has always been
At home in Paradise Way
For here I retire, never to return
To the illusion of separate days
Time will exist no longer I find
The day we know we never die

The Promise

Last night as I lay
Ready for sleep at last
A visitor joined me there
In silent greeting stayed
No words were ever spoken
No thoughts to get in the way
Of the joining there taking place
Upon my bed at end of day
My silent friend did impose upon me
All that I ever prayed for
As we lay in perfect union
I never thought to ask for more
My beloved friend stayed but for an instant
Eternity would have suited me well
But he left behind the promise
Of which I cannot say
Not because I deemed it secret
But only because words could never say
What was truly promised
In my bed, to me, that day

Various Ways

These poems I write
I would truly love to share
With all my beloved brothers
For whom I deeply care
They are truly gifts from Heaven
Sent in various ways
Each a gentle blessing
Touching me on sundry days
I know not their intended home
Or if they are to stay
Resident within these pages
Or distributed in assorted ways
I need only remember
Tis not my direction to say
That choice belongs to Holy Spirit
For Him to decide in His holy way

High All the Time

I really do enjoy
The place and time I go
In elevated state of mind
Getting high most of the time
Tooling about in cerebral cubby
Looking for wonders of mind
I'm digging the state of mind I'm in
Staying high much of the time
Wondrous worlds never imagined
Within, without, lightly touched
Wafting through on amber breezes
Soaring high nearly all of the time
It reminds me quite frankly
Of days gone by
In haze-filtered byways
When drugs were my buds
Now I'm doing it au natural
No LSD or nose candy around
Staying high all of the time
Best buzz I ever found

Blind Enough To See

I pray for the day
When I am blind enough to see
Past my brothers
As bodies before me
To everything shaded as nothing
In this most superficial place
To deny all separate parts that implore me
To listen to lies without end
Vision uncompromised is left me
Sweet clarity of love revealed
To see with unlimited wisdom
That which lies before me
As treasure, my one true fate

Ego Gift Declined

The ego denies us many things
Heaven's gifts among those banned
Offered in place of divinity declined
Trinkets and baubles to detain
From treasure of worth untouched
Specialness granted as agent
To justify not being as one
To be better at this or that
Or brighter or taller or richer
Anything to make me other than you
Excuses granted for defense and attack
These evil toys are given
Not to enrich or extol
Merely means to an unholy end
Making us fragmented and weak
Turn away from such false impressions
And know we are all the same
Not special just holy, my friend
With Paradise our gain

Ring of Truth

The sound of truth rings clearly
Finding home in mind of man
Striking chords well hidden
Resonating at long last
A host of words read and spoken
Most rang hollow and held no merit
Steps on the pathway misunderstood
Minute course corrections unnoticed
Meaningless provisions turned to angels
To keep us from staying lost
Keeping us pointed in due direction
Until said day arrives
When in our path before us
We witness truth become our friend
Neither science nor curriculum need verify
The thing we know as real
The Christ within will recognize
And distinguish celestial bells
As mind reverberates in wonder
At the ring of truth revealed

Brothers Without Arms

Uncle Abe, surround us
With wholeness your vision knew
Worthy soul to step forth
And heal the open wounds
Even the founding fathers
Found no time to cure
The evil that plagued our people
And forbade us from being pure
The promise of America never realized
Until fateful days had passed
That sadly spilled our blood en masse
Yet one brother deserves another
And none must kneel down
To anything less than Creator
So fight we did in countless regret
Let hate become our creed
Then you brought love to heal us
And make us one again
Our country and soul indebted
To you Mr. President departed
For healing our wounds and restoring
Our souls as born anew
Eloquent words and daring acts
Intended to reunite
Brothers black and white
Under the symbol of unity
Colored red, white, and blue
But in truth you were directed
As voice and words rang true
By gentle Creator's will
To be brothers in arms no more
Though anger and rage played out
On battlefields large and small
Once the wounds were healed
Love became our battle cry
And brotherhood the prize

Mr. Obama, If You Please

Mr. Obama, if you please
Look me in the eye and show me
That light or darkness lie below
Regardless of reflection shown
You will be the soul
We look within to find our own
Since I speak only truth
As well as I know
I look to you as earthly captain
A rallying point for brothers lost
A center to become around
A lightening rod of attention
No room allowed for fences still
So stand tall my young brother
Brave heart may you be blessed
Our Father's holy covenant
Bestowed at your request
A purpose to raise us all
As one people to serve the rest

Nothing Left To Chance

I see the world quite differently
I hope someday you will too
Though at times it may seem quite interesting
In truth it will never do
It has its ups and downs
Its aches and pains to be sure
This mixed bag of offerings
Not good enough for you
Let us discard the coin of chance
And place our faith where it belongs
In the love our Father holds for us
In a place where we always dance
Where joy is the music played
And nothing is left to chance

Skinny Sister

Bare bones beauty
Still not fair enough
Getting skinnier to be more loved
Shrinking away to less than you are
If beauty be in the eye of the beholder
Then sweet sister, you are blind
No sacrifice needed or asked for
To be admired by dearest Self
No need to keep subtracting
Pounds away from flesh
Love will only come from disappearing
Into our Father's faith
Your sentence is done little sister
All penance due has been paid
Stand up now and be proud
Of the beautiful creature within
No more denigration allowed

The Perfect Home

I merit no punishment
Nor call to vengeance
I have done nothing to regret
I see no reason for guilt
No cause for denunciation
Time for disease and pain to cease
Weapons against self no longer
I need only to know and forgive
All that never was
For fall into a dream we did
A nightmare of major extent
Nothing compared to waking state
Where sin is known as naught
Hard to grasp this must be
For minds so long in chains
We remain but innocent creatures
Disguised in the world as less
But less we have never been
Though sad is surely true
For we have missed our innocence lost
Yet while a thing is missing
It surely must continue to be
In the place it always was
Waiting to be found and freed
Lost in the myth of separation and sin
Punishing with both without end
Someday we will awake my brothers
To know the purity we own
Never again to merit retribution
Safe forever in the perfect home

No Need for Need

There is nothing to gain
And nothing to lose
For you see, we have it all
Everything for eternity
No cause for concern
No need to conceal
That which we treasure
And believe we need
So build no vaults
Or fences to protect
Those meager belongings
That we hold in such regret
Poverty resides first in mind
Then reflects in form denied
No need to covet what we lack
No requirement to hoard or save
The only need to eliminate
The greed that covets the grave
Sacrifice and lack starve our soul
Confines our belief to what we see
Let us move beyond such blindness
And be greeted by all we can be
Awaiting our return to vision
Poised to grant us all
Divine gifts far exceeding
Anything owned in form
No longer willing to replace
The frail for the strong
The incomplete for the whole
Eyes wide open to deny
The ego in exchange for the soul
The treasure unending and eternal
Of God's gifts given so freely
Replacing His Son's meager effects
With those of love and peace

You may purchase these not
With dollars made or stolen
They are free and of utmost value
So lay down the thought of insufficiency
Accept what is offered for all
No sacrifice intended or required
Just give what is received
All of us sharing everything
All that we own as need
Open up the vaulted storehouse
That guarantees your greed
Open the mind to abundance
To our Father's precious relief
Put aside all theft of giving
No need to only receive
All that is given is boundless
To be shared our only need

As I Go

As I depart this time and place
Remember me kindly amid a smile
We have touched each other briefly
And shared some time as one
Pointed in mutual direction
Guided by goals we owned
The work was done
And quite well it appears
Task complete and ended
We walked together
And we talked together
And now we must move apart
You in your way
Me in mine
Forever in each others heart

Those I Have Known

For those I have known
And those I have not
The faces I remember
The names I forgot
Only placards to remind us
Of time spent wisely in accord
In time and space as home
Know that I have ever known you
And you forever me
Born on the same day and occasion
Of holy Parent, we three
Brothers and sisters briefly lost
Placed apart by world of opposites
Facing off against each other
Forgetting what once was shared
Fighting endless battles in unison
Nothing but pain our prize
But through the strife and time apart
We have never forgotten to remember
The love that lives in our hearts
The ever present thing that joins us
And never lets us forget
That one we are in truth
No matter our path or fate
Let us touch that truth together
Push aside all that hates
For we have known each other forever
And will again some day

All or Nothing

Your wish is your belief
And belief begets form
Believe in scarcity
Make insufficiency your reward
Make abundance your vision
Allow that treasure to come
The need for nothing
Ownership in the All
Obviates lesser forms
Makes us richest of all
Poverty is a disease of mind
A deficit of faith involved
Yet treasure and riches abound
When faith brings abundance along

Poet Restrained

I am not yet published
Writer and poet in practice only
All treasures delivered yet to me
Unable to share what must be shared
Its nature beguiles me
To join its purpose and goal
The will to connect all participants
Who come to heal their wounds
The letters and words and constructs
My best food prepared and given
To bring across the love-sealed messages
That beckons us home forthwith
Demonstrating its inclusive nature
Attraction to all, withheld from none
Bidding us join the club
Of fellow Christ souls assembled
To gain entry of the door
That allows only One to enter

Mountain of a Lady

You are a mountain of a lady
In so many different ways
Wide of girth and mind
Larger than life around you
No time approved for distractions
None needed if all are included
In the family of workers you pay
And they are it seems dear lady
Mother to them all you are
A firm but fair distributor
Of love prodded by eagerness required
For the position held as lamppost
And source of begotten praise
I know you worthy lady
At levels never displayed
Your heart is pure
Your worth is gold
Lead on in inclusive fashion
Making blessed union your goal

Each Our Own

I can wait no longer
Too long apart we have been
Incomplete for countless ages
Ever since time began
I can be here no longer
Unless I be with you
My long lost beloved brother
Let fear no longer separate
Nor guilt be our mutual guest
Lay aside all that hinders
And precludes our very best
For we are nothing apart dear brother
And everything when joined
Wandering, once lost in the desert
Now found by each our own

Trinity

Knowledge eternal now revealed
To waiting mind long confused
Burdened by guilt and injustice
Unable to see what was always true
Blinded by the grand illusion
The band of brothers denied
Blighted by tiny beliefs divided
Unable to overlook what never was
The original sin that never happened
The guilt and pain of that simple act
Burying us in a world of lies
Yet our Beloved never leaves us
Without comfort or love to reveal
The truth of innocence never lost
No need to attack ourselves or others
Simply forgive what never was or is
The Beloved still awaits us
Hoping to join us from within
All children gathered in Holy Ghost
The Three now One again

Perfection Restrained

The world refuses to grant perfection
Only the vain pursuit of it allowed
It cannot depict it accurately
Or accept its wholeness unbound
It may only dream about it
In distant dimming view
As a dream held within a dream
Of vision's golden dawn
Perfection could never reside here
The accommodations far too shabby
No arrangements possible to permit
Its occupancy within
Yet something gnaws at the memory
Of brighter days gone by
The pull of the distant light
Draws us nigh to perfection's door
Throwing off the chains that restrain us
Becoming our Self once more

Simplicity of Union

We are Mind
And nothing less
Confused for awhile
By bodies imagined
The thought of separation
Born to distract
From truth of oneness
Always fact
Nothing to rejoin
Nothing gone astray
Vision briefly obscured
By the dream's allure
Nothing seen in eye exists
Separate things, toys of illusion
One Mind we will always be
The dream composed in total
Of pain and fear and misery
All born to blind and separate
From oneness Heaven born
Close our eyes to see
The simplicity of union
And the certainty of love
Look past the gap that lies
To us in so many ways
Look not down or sideways
As we cross the bridge uniting
Lost souls bound in life eternal

The Last Fairy Tale

This will surely be
The last fairy tale I read
Characters played by brothers
In myth upon stage of dreams
For the roles we play are simply that
A script, a character, in myth
No more to be distracted about
All that amuses and enthralls
I can no longer believe it
Even as trifle in the wind
No longer will it entertain me
With illusions replacing the genuine
For truth is so much larger
Amid story so well-told
A story of such magnitude
No room for idle imaginings
What need have I of such trinkets
When replaced by riches unbound
What interest commands my mind
When the universe challenges it so
So I put aside the fantasy
That has captured and ravaged my soul
Turning now only to reality
Putting aside what no longer delights
Merging my mind in all its wonder
With my brothers' in soothing light
Minds joined in holy wedlock
Telling true stories of Paradise

Naked Prize

I cannot go before my brothers in infirmity
And proclaim I have found my way
For in truth I have not until I can say
What stands before you as witness
Is blameless in every way
The truth of what I am
Must show in blinding light
Nothing concealed or out of sight
I must be as I assert
The words are not enough
A standing presence and tribute provided
To separation denied and oneness claimed
Purity must be my bequest
Shared in what I say
But an argument far less convincing
Than being what I pray
So I come before you dear brother
Shed of all that would hide
Naked in my innocence
With promise to share my prize

One Mind

One Mind between us
Beloved brother Christ
Now I reach out
To share it with all
The ultimate gift given
From you to my fallen self
Raising me up to Heaven
Devoid of all I left
My purpose now fully defined
The charter at last prepared
To provide all that is given
With the same Mind
We all share

Love Makes Me Cry

Love makes me cry
And I don't know why
Its beauty and glow fill me
With feeling unworldly
A gift from God no doubt
Reminder of oneness forgotten
The aroma of true identity
A gift worth receiving and living
So why does it make me weep
Do I deem myself unworthy
Or regret what I thought I lost
Or simply because it fills me
With God my Father at last
I may not know for a moment
Certainty may bid me wait
But cry or laugh with joy no matter
I accept and cherish my fate
As my Father bestows upon me
All that would make me great

Flute Divine

The old man waits, only to offer
What Christ would have him play
He shines his diamond heart my way
And asks which tune I will play
On flute given to sound the way
Whatever song my savior renders
Shall leave my lips delightfully
At Holy Spirit's request
Life lived long only to be
At this time and place
Waiting simply to hear
What I need offer in tribute
To what life holds dear
And would surely dispel my fear
A simple tune is all I need tender
Of love and grace displayed
A melody from Heaven composed
To sooth and voice the way
To attract my brother to me
That travel home we may

Seekers of Common Thread

The only way to find the truth
Is to look beyond all that lies
To ignore what seeks to confuse
And place among us the divide
That blinds to what endures
And seeks to hide our oneness
To forgive is not to dishonor
Intentions from hearts so pure
But refusal to see what keeps us
Apart and ourselves untrue
Disbelieve all that hinders
All that would lie in our way
Of knowing who we are
And sharing what we may
Of the divine love presented
That unites us one and all
Look through counterfeit fog
To revealing light ahead
To truth discovered in total
All seekers of common thread

Sacrifice Poker

I recently played the sacrifice card
In a game rigged to reveal
Collection of thoughts intended
To attack and then conceal
Motives less than pure
And target undeserving
The need to believe in sacrifice
The only evidence required
To defend attack upon
The Christ unduly masqueraded
Poor me now justified
In proceeding with my plan
To unleash guilt and anger
Upon my fellow man
Righteous now in self-defending
The attack so rightly rendered
Projecting all deception believed
Upon my holy sister
Making more of what never was
Attempting to make her less
The ego drive to divide and conquer
Given leave to strike and harm
Putting upon my brother's intention
Only what I would believe
Making her wrong at all costs
To make me right instead
Giving pause and cause to tender
My guilt upon her head
The hidden motive so impure
To keep us all apart
By taking guilt from my endeavor
And placing it in brother's heart

The Forgiveness Game

I think I may finally get it
What forgiveness truly means
Not letting go of injury or slight
Instead simply ignoring
The scene of deception unending
From mind's concealing door
That houses the tiny tyrant
That seeks to make us poor
Guilt and anger its jagged tools
Giving rise to projection's cause
The unholy mental mechanism
That hopes to give us pause
In due consideration of unity
And oneness divinely bestowed
The mental flaw used destructively
To transfer guilt and shame
To brother considered unequal
And certainly the one to blame
For all of our fear and uncertainty
The target of the unholy game
Making our brother wrong
Certainly the gist of the same
Unloading all that we blatantly deny
Falling to us to claim
The transfer complete
The dream game is won
Attack upon our selves proceeds
Both losers in this guilty game
Let us resign our positions
And leave chimera behind
Simply overlook it
In favor of truth in time
A losers game to be sure
Not fit for holy contender
Let us plainly discard it
And forgive what never was

BFF

In time I justly discover
The friend sought forever
Lost and missing part of soul
Thought never to be mine again
The friend with whom I could share
All that lay hidden within
The one true confidante
To receive my heart's poetry
The tender offerings so long concealed
The truth so much in need
Of sharing with trusted brother
I see quite clearly now
The holy sibling has lived within
Ever a part of soul divine
The Christ eternal my friend
Best friend forever
In all good souls before me

Perfect Ground

I find myself here alone
Wondering why I have not arrived
At Heaven's door and goal achieved
Realizing at once I have not forgiven
The progress I seek and unfulfilled
This once I look behind me
To see from whence I have come
And see the distance traveled
From lost soul to Christ now known
I pause but for a moment
To know what I have imposed
Upon my soul well traveled
To discern and then forgive
For destination not yet gained
My quest for complete forgiveness
Blocked by none but myself
Time to cut myself some slack
And cherish how far I've come
Closer to King and Brother now
I draw near to perfect ground

Less Road Ahead Than Behind

Seek not perfection
For it was never lost
But rather welcome forgiveness
For not finding what cannot be found
Truly an imperfect world we live in
Not our home by any means
We have traveled long and far
To arrive to where we started
Pat yourself on the back dear brother
And know how far you've come
Perfection forgotten but never lost
One more bridge and we're home

Nothing But Oneness

I have found my home
It is not here or there
But everywhere
Not with this person or that
With every man, woman, and child
With the living thing
That runs through all living things
Well-cozied in eternity
The universe my home
Wrapped in the arms of my Father
Warmed by Heaven's glow
Surrounded on every side
By love's gentle heart
Nothing but oneness
And never apart

Our Will Be Done

Partners all, though unknown
Component pieces of a whole
Minus lines and delineation
All in One, One in All
A common will between us
The love that becomes us
Indistinguishable from the All
One mind of many presented
As something less than needed
When access to them all is inherited
Never apart, only separately interested
In an idea that could only be conceived
In mind less than whole and un-freed
For in truth we are simply one
One mind and spirit all
No need for dissent or disagreement
Or arguing with ourselves at all

Writer, Poet, Friend

A writer, a poet, a friend
A point from which to begin
Worthy trades all and bringing
Comfort and joy within
A life's work spent on other things
Well attempted with love's complement
A vocation though not a passion
Delivers me here at glory's gate
Presented with options so inviting
I cannot but stop and think
How much I must be loved
How grand we all must be
Let me lend a hand my friend
Let my heart sing you some lines
Of poetry lovingly written
That brings your heart to mine

Alternative Fruit

I reject all idols large and small
I need them not
They are nothing at all
A multitude of fossils presented
Since the beginning of time
Distract us well they do
And blind us to the truth
Yet purity of thought and being
Offered as alternative fruit

The Tower of Babble

Different languages in different terms
Words with different meanings
Interpretations changing perception
All intended for confusion's sake
No way to communicate
No path to take together
Wondering aimlessly in varying direction
Unable to commune or relate
A world that breeds such confusion
And refuses to let us be one
Certainly provides no comfort
No sanctuary to be safe
Deny these differences we must
If sanity be our goal
Look for deeper meaning
Something built for hope
Look to love to simplify
And Heaven to light the way
To a place where all is clarity
Where communication is not what we say
But rather a knowing that does defy
All that we see here
With perception that tells us lies
Let simple truth be our guiding light
Replacing chaos with certainty found
Living together in oneness
With no confusion allowed
Sweet peace and contentment
Surround when separation departs
No longer spinning aimlessly
Remaining home in divine heart

?

It's different, what can I say
Shows its colors in an alternative way
As different as night and day
Nothing to compare to
Unique in every way
A provincial offering made
An invitation to come and see
This thing that no one made
Indescribable at best
Unavoidable at least
No reference or cipher will do
The truth of it evades us
While stunned by its magnificence
Look simply to its essence
No definition required to explain
The beauty and elegance of its simplicity
Involved in Mind, devoid of pain

Lines of Distinction

Stretching higher and sinking lower
Seeking thrills from other lands
Pushing hard to burst constraint
Beyond the lines of distinction
A sullied dark secret, yes
Yet the impulse is quite clear
To go beyond our seamless straits
Merging again in lineless states
Pushing beyond the borders
Trying hard to eliminate
Those lines of distinction
That determines our fate
Boundless now, ever so
Tearing down walls and mirrors
Releasing freedom's long wait
Lines of distinction now fading
Having led us to Heaven's gate

Choose Again

Periods of illness upon us
Following a life's endeavor
Older age provides us license
To settle in and self-convince
That body so long and well-honored
Seeks to betray us again
Slowing becoming our reality
Gaining stature at mind's expense
Until it becomes us wholly
Mind reduced to brain our sin
The form so adored and hated
For what it is and contradicts
Lost in the storm of sensation
Our life reduced to this
Rampant emotions mixed with pain
Convincing of material dominance
Dismissing the sanctity of Mind
Leaving room for fear and doubt
Confining us to body and emotion
Obscuring the only way out
Years of pain and suffering
Diseases and broken bones
All of the package offered
All that we believe we own
Yet the Mind can never vanish
Or the Spirit it calls its home
Both waiting behind the curtain
To be claimed some day alone
For when we tire of sickness
And know there must be more
Then turn our love and attention
To God of whom we're born
His love and radiance will show us
How much more we are than form
We choose again my brother
To be healed and leave the storm

I Write Like a Crazy Man

I write like a crazy man today
Surrounded by this and that
Bombarded by senses and things
That sparkle, glisten, and die
Inside or out I know not
Mind's infant or worldly praise
Truth beckons to stay within
Ignore the frail flack
Ideas less than ennobled
Flying about without constraint
Empty distractions indeed
Amounting to less than nothing
Failing to sustain or feed
No food for the soul
No light for the mind
Errant orphans from ego's breast
Lacking any real importance
Indistinguishable from the rest
Let me be free to ignore them
Let only one Voice put me at rest

Providence Understands

Who decides of literary triumph
Or digs the obscure grave
To let the words rise to the heavens
Or lie beneath the feet of men
I like to think it be providence
That makes such thoughts of import
Men know not what they need
And I among them
Leave such concerns to destiny
Where better decisions are earned
Understand we know so little
Of what will make us complete
Leave it to our Maker
And learn what arrives at hand
Have trust that what becomes us
Is all we need to stand
Before our brothers in unison
And say "I understand"

The World is False

The world is false
And everything in it
Differences and things abound
Better or worse, right or wrong
Good or bad, up or down
All bode for separation
The greatest illusion of all
Truth is One my friends
Peace, certainty, and joy
Wholeness, freedom, undying life
All one and shared between us
No division possible
Nothing to take
Nothing to give
All communal, no reason to clash
Truth and knowledge known by all
No sickness, wars, or hate
No jealousy, envy, or lust
No illness in any form
Only one choice to be made
Truth or illusion, life or death

Ultimate Facts

The ultimate facts are upon us
Nothing left to arrange or compile
No need left for analysis
Acceptance the only criteria
For learning what needs to be known
Let go all the statisticians
Leave the spin for lesser ways
Continue not false impressions
No manipulation involved at all
Insight requires some housekeeping
Removal of debris required
Make room for superior knowledge
Clean until purity shines
Laying gold upon the flooring
Providing ample room to kneel
At sumptuous alter before me
Mind and heart opened wide
To receive and accept what is mine

Examples of Perfection

I see examples of perfection
Amid moments hid from view
In finer arenas than visible
They show me God exists
Love lives in their center
Sharing itself with one and all
All who come to see it
With naked eyes and open heart
Innocence recalled from distant past
To wrap the sacred idea
In love long forgotten
But now a holy shield
From all that tries to impress us
With fractured facts and false ideas
They attack our mind relentlessly
But suffer them no ill
They are but weak and shadowy specters
Who cannot pierce the shield
Let the imperfect lie
They hold no place in life
Replaced by moments of perfection
Embraced by Father's love
Waiting to bestow upon us
The glory of sweet excellence
The calmness of peace at rest
Eternal freedom and wholeness
All the examples we need
The entirety subsumed at last

Pleasure's Mask

Pain in pleasure's garb
The world's offerings laid before me
The sacrifice required not evident
No price displayed or conveyed
Yet costly indeed the acceptance
Everything for nothing the exchange
World and its king, the body
Setting price and conditions alike
Demanding false obedience
And debt never-ending
Fame and fortune and pleasure the booty
Hollow offerings all
Traded for peace and freedom
And denial of Heaven's call
Dreams will manifest hidden desires
And make a life to pursue them
To fruitless endeavor they fall
No more chance of success is offered
Unless we decide not to awake
And ask ourselves if dreams be our goal
If peace of Heaven be the stakes

And He Says Yes

Our Creator offers us a deal
Everything for nothing the prize
And we say "Everything for nothing?"
And He says "Yes"
But we hesitate ever so slightly
A moment taken to contemplate
All that we might lose and give up
And could trickery be involved
Could deception be afoot
Is this deal too good to be true
Maybe we should settle for less
Just to be safe, you know
Maybe nothing for everything isn't so bad
Let's take a seat and think about it

No More Blah, Blah, Blah

No more blah, blah, blah
Get to the point my friend
Just spit it out in solid solution
The essence only if you please
So many words with sole intent
Of obscuring all that is sent
Essential gifts bright glowing
Shaded by language well spun
No more half-knowing for me
Cut to the chase I will
Down to the heart of the matter
No matter what it seems
And when I finally discover
The heart of gold within
The lovely gem I've been given
Language will no longer win

Heaven's Gate

I have written down my children for you
Committed them to paper I have
These gifts of joy bestowed upon me
Now to share with you my friend
My family is your family now
Brothers we truly are
God has sent us angels
They come to take us far
Away from this lesser place
To our home original built
Both of us and our children
Together at Heaven's Gate

More Than My Skin

I am more than my skin
Let me out, let me in
Dwarfed by buckets of rain
Cleansing below for changelings
Out of the way I'm sure
Filling a thimble with the ocean
Is no small feat for man
Might need a little assistance
Someone to hold your hand
So as to keep it steady
Avoid any shake or tremble
Never miss a drop into
That holy little thimble

Words Are Not Enough

Words are not enough
My heart expands from love
For He who made me
And my family born above
My holy brother and best friend
Teacher, poet, and myself
The Holy Spirit, my beloved Captain
Who guides my soul to its end
My dearest Father, creator of all
Who loves me fiercely and gently
All so much a part of the other
The thought of it takes me to tears
To know I am safe and eternal
Gives such pause to make me think
Perhaps I need no words at all

Nothing Fragile Here

There is nothing fragile about this art
It arrives both day and night
Appears in various states of mind
Early times or late no matter
The connection quite firm now
No particular setting required
My Brother and I now attuned
To the work we share and do
He delivers from the Source He abides in
I receive with grateful mind
The pen simply following orders
Putting ink to paper as scribe
The gifts delivered for poetry's sake
Wrapped in words so lovely and fine
Handed to you my brother
To abide with you in time
To someday make a difference
And gently prod you home to stay
Join me on the path my friend
Let us retrace the gift's traveled way

Forty Times Two

I will live to be eighty
The last quadrant I enter now
Much will happen in mid-stance
As I grow older and holier
Graying hair heralds, I even look the part
Of worldly writer waiting to wane
But neither is the truth of me
This aged vehicle no longer vital
To knowing the authentic I
Speed and endurance no longer issues
I stay where I am and emit
All signals passed through me
Receiving with all the rest
Pearls of wisdom and joy engendered
Such blessings never guessed
Stand tall old man
Give the best of your time
Moved along by angel's means
No reason to worry
No time to pine

The Feast

More upon more this will fade
Material trappings, trapping indeed
Finer things anticipate exploring
Sumptuous feast awaits
We need only refine our appetite
For food less course and fallible
Close your eyes, awake thereafter
The dream much poorer than truth
Mealy meal offered instead
Lesser fare served ahead
Turn away from the obvious
Lean towards Spirit's being
Waded through the swamp to get here
No time to abate in fear
Press on through the darkness
Let faith carry on splendid wings
Homeward to Heaven's Feast

My Only Fate

If it be of you Father
Then I surely welcome it in
No need for identification
The heart holds no door
The mind open and awake
Any and all from you Father
Of this I cannot wait
I need to be whole within You
This my only fate

Metamorphosis Benediction

I will let no weak deceptions
Rule me or bar the way
To the birth that soon awaits me
Transcendence of womb desired
To awake in silent state
Peace and love surrounding
The cradle of the dove
Aware and awake at long last
Singing benedictions out loud
To sweet metamorphosis allowed

Wisdom Speaks Softly

I would not reclaim a minute
Of time spent wisely so
Listening for whispers
Wanting it to be so
Hoping Love speaks ever so slowly
To savor each moment as one
Hearing angel chimes at distance
The sunrise offering its notes
Christ speaks in thought
Wisdom voiced so softly
In gifts that can't be bought

Table Scraps

No more settling for scraps
When the feast lies just ahead
No more trimmings or baubles
No more settling for less
Look beyond the bait to the trap
And further still to table laden
Seductive and taunting they be
These insignificant frills
Be they sex or money or approval
They grip and hold for life
Draining the fire from our will
Dampening the desire to fulfill
Turning us to thumb-sucking babies
When wise and powerful we are
Reducing our reality to dim potential
Sparing our eyes from the sun
Buying us for a sixpence
Mortgaging our soul for one
They come around whenever
The portal to truth may part
Taking no chances whatsoever
That love will pierce our heart
Allowing fame and fortune
To overshadow all that is owned
Pennies at our feet to distract us
From Paradise pouring blessings
Upon our hallowed heads
Sons of God we are my friends
Princes of the universe within
Kneel down to no seduction
Head held high in recognition
Of Creator and worthy Friend

Brother Walt

The words bleed from my soul
Spirit emanating from divine center
Taking hold of all above it
Beckoning residents in between
Just got through reading Whitman
Sparked by restless fire
Elevated to parts unknown
Brother Walt the same as I
He and the band of brothers know it
All connected by the poet's song
Dare we be channel and spout
For that which feeds the soul
And consumes us entirely
Begging us to listen acutely
To soul song rendered by love
Of Father to blessed Son

Saying Goodbye to T&A

For the most part
I engage my brother rightly
Yet in sister's form
Something stands in the way
Body parts far too appealing
Distract from direction desired
Pulling mind back to baser things
Let me be blunt, all things considered
I will say what needs to be said
We recurrently yield to bodily attractions
Though obstacles they may be
Mind bent towards matter
Navigates spirit away
Preoccupation with boobies and buttocks
Such a silly diversion
To deaden fair minds that way
What draws us to such protuberances
When but mounds of flesh they are
Wasting so much of attention
When holiness beckons from afar
I think sometimes
We cannot be
Both divine and so amused
By fleshy bumps and curves
How can mind so fair
Be split so far asunder
And be landlord to both
And not ever wonder
Why something so insignificant
Can divert us from Heaven's door
The body, a symbol since time began
Of separation made evident
Handmaiden to guilt and shame
Yet magnet to pull us away
From destiny much grander

Than body parts in play
So commonplace and well-accepted
Only the most puritanical complain
We allow the images to fill the void
And be deceived about our pain
Our mind deserves so much more
Than given by naked prey
Admit our intent of what we desire
And decide if it be our way
The body so historically used
To seduce and lead astray
From mind so sadly diluted
At last, to fall away
From fate much more deserving
Of what we bring to bear
On lives so thinly lived
And souls that never care
Awake we will someday
To the cost of where mind plays
There to put all semblance of
Boobies and buttocks away

What My Soul Yearns

We decide, do we not
What we do with one another
So long appraised of lonely tasks
I can only stop and wonder
Where confidence led
And put asunder
All notions of things done rightly
No assurance now of past well-followed
No faith in separate things
Only safe decisions now
From mind merged to brothers lightly
I make no decisions apart from truth
My will surrendered so blithely
To far larger concerns
I turn attention prescribed
To those I know and confirm
No longer young or confident
In worldly ways well-learned
Care now only given
To what my soul still yearns

Separation Anxiety

I leave now this place so slightly visited
My stay not long at all
A worthy time and place to be
Time spent with friends so fair
I place my fate in One far wiser
Who will take me to life's next door
So sad to leave those hardly known
Yet we all move on to new locales
To meet our destined workings
We touched each other in ways unknown
We enjoyed our moments shared
But now time has informed us
We are to be together no more
Forget not soon brothers and sisters
How rich the moments chimed
Bringing us together all too briefly
To share a point in time
I feel uneasy as I prepare
To leave this place I've been
Wondering if I fully accounted
For the gift of you, my friends

Enhanced Interrogation

The world we call our home
Is a shabby place indeed
The ones whom we elect to govern
Shame us repeatedly
All in the name of patriotism
When in fact it is only fear
That drives us to commit
Unspeakable acts of misery
Let us demand our honor back
And let the world take note
That harm by any other name
Still corrupts our soul
The quest to be biggest and best
Is lost as hate takes its toll
I would rather be dead than dishonored
Spirit intact, nobody's fool
Time to destroy all excuses
That gives us leave to demean
No more rationale for torture
No more sacrifice of soul
Let us leave enhanced interrogation
To those who do not claim
To be a land of freedom
And home of liberty's flame

Dying to Live

Prevention for this, treatment for that
Take some more vitamins
Eat some more fruit
Watch out for those microbes
Best to avoid human touch
Wash the hands when opportune
The cure for mine is the bane of yours
Side effects abound and threaten
One day a likely villain
The next a miracle cure
Better watch out for the next bad thing
And ignore the fear below
Never question why none works for all
Nor a world obsessed with health
Spending so many minutes and dollars
To stave off the inevitable death
A quest for immortality
Masked by health concerns
Nothing consistent, nothing new
Only the appeal to fear universal
If nothing works as advertised
Can it truly be true
Perhaps we are missing a factor
Perhaps we look too far
Dare we stop to consider
The cause of the symptom's core
Will mind lend a useful clue
Is it possible it forecasts our world
Projecting ill thoughts and diseases
Then misleading the means to heal
Consider for one brief moment
That all comes from mind
Joy, peace, and happiness
Along with sickness we find
To assuage the guilt we expect

And punishment we think we deserve
Everything that plagues us
Fruit of the mind disturbed
So let us stop our pursuit of life
Simply live it the best we can
Have faith that good thoughts will attend us
And show us eternity's plan
Let go the fear that drives us
To seek where naught is found
No remedy or potion available
To protect us from the sound
Of death steadily approaching
Look inward for lasting health
Only Mind can make us well

Young Brother

Straight and smart and upward bound
The path you follow unknown
Lean on ways of being
Honest, fair, and strong
Intellect can be both friend and foe
More than a brain
More than you know
The mind is mysterious
And defies our attempts
To master its mettle
Or know its bounds
Intelligence is more far-reaching
Than gathering of facts
A limitless knowing beyond our own
The wisest of the wise
Will surely pronounce
The sign of intelligence true
Is knowing how little we know
It matters much more what we do
So walk your path with humility
And decrement no fellow mind
And yours will serve you well
No matter what you find
Learn from all who will show you
The part of mind they grow
Mature in mind and spirit
And worry not where you go
And if we ever meet again
You can tell me what you know

Fair Indian Prince

Young man going through prime of life
Gathering knowledge as you go
Giving your all to profession
Sharing the best that you know
A job well done your legacy
I can see all it pervades
Walk your path in princely stride
Ennoble all you do and create
Make the most of your time on earth
I recognize that you do
And never forget those who enjoyed you
Count me among them too

Boss Lady

It has truly been an event
This short time between us
An interval well spent
I will miss your humor and warmth
The respect of human worth
The toughness and gentleness
Mixed well in leader's girth
I wish you well
And hope you will find
A cure for the pain that pales you
An obstacle well known
And crossed by myself
I know where it will find you
Let it not claim your soul
For your worth is far too great
And your time yet unknown
Let the love that abides you
Shape what you will share
Include those all around you
Those fortunate in your care

Poet's Doubt

What a meek and deserving occasion
This time spent well-written
Molding words and phrases
Reflecting ideas not yet born
Speaking lightly, still not knowing
If what we say be true
Vague notions and sultry ideas
Feeling right about it
The only evidence of truth revealed
I challenge my own inspiration
Being so newborn to its taste
Yet trust carries me on
Faith comforts me fairly
And moves my pen further
Letting the words surprise themselves
Landing without warning
Stretching mind fabric and garments
Filling voids where they live
Casting doubt on fixed beliefs
If this be our purpose
Let us continue unencumbered
Dare to be boundless and agile
Write on with courage brother scribe
The poet's pen is not your own
Merely rented for temporal reasons
Paper still requires the inking
Of thoughts purely loaned
Welcome it when words are no longer needed
Nor discrete ideas partially dissected
Parsed for presentation
To minds divided so

www.ingramcontent.com/pod-product-compliance
Lightning Source LLC
Chambersburg PA
CBHW070918160426
43193CB00011B/1517